Daily Activity Bank

SOCIAL STUDIES

SCOTT FORESMAN

THE WORLD

PEARSON

Scott
Foresman

Editorial Offices: Glenview, Illinois • Parsippany, New Jersey • New York, New York
Sales Offices: Parsippany, New Jersey • Duluth, Georgia • Glenview, Illinois
Coppell, Texas • Ontario, California

www.sfsocialstudies.com

MW01612860

Contents

ISBN 0-328-03927-6

Copyright © Pearson Education, Inc.
All rights reserved. Printed in the United States of America. The blackline masters in this publication are designed for use with appropriate equipment to reproduce copies for classroom use only. Scott Foresman grants permission to classroom teachers to reproduce these masters.

5 6 7 8 9 10 V008 10 09 08 07 06 05

Fast Fact 1

Alexander the Great's empire stretched all the way from Greece, through Egypt, to India.

On which continents was Alexander the Great's empire located?

Geography

History

Fast Fact 2

During the last Ice Age, glaciers covered about one-third of the Earth's surface.

When did the last Ice Age end?

Fast Fact 3

Currency in Costa Rica is called the *colón*. It is named after Christopher Columbus, whose name in Spanish is *Cristóbal Colón*.

Who funded Christopher Columbus on his exploration, and for what reasons?

Economics

Government
Citizenship

Fast Fact 4

The ancient Egyptians and Chinese were the first civilizations to use postal systems.

How did the Inca send important messages throughout the empire?

Fast Fact 5

The ancient Greeks held the first Olympic Games. The games were so important to the Greek people that time was measured in _Olmpiads,_ the four-year intervals between games.

When do we celebrate the modern Olympic Games?

Culture

Geography

Fast Fact 6

The Vinson Massif is the highest peak in Antarctica.

How many tourists visit Antarctica in an average year?

Fast Fact 7

Sumerians used sophisticated calendars to measure time. Each calendar day had twelve periods, and each of these periods was broken down into thirty parts of about four minutes.

Where did civilizations first develop?

History

Economics

Fast Fact 8

Linen cloth, which is made of fibers from the flax plant, is one of the oldest known textiles.

How did women in the Zhou dynasty make silk cloth?

Fast Fact 9

In ancient Rome, the emperor granted citizenship to foreigners as a reward for military service.

How did Roman soldiers prove their citizenship?

Government Citizenship

Culture

Fast Fact 10

People first drank tea in China in about 2700 B.C.

Name two other important products developed in China.

Fast Fact 11

The Caspian Sea is the world's largest saltwater lake and a major source of caviar.

What countries border the Caspian Sea?

Geography

History

Fast Fact 12

Some Asian armies used elephants to frighten their enemies and break down defensive walls.

What Carthaginian general crossed the Alps with his troops and a herd of elephants during the Punic Wars?

Fast Fact 13

American Don Wetzel invented the automated teller machine, also called an ATM or a cash machine, in 1969.

What is the purpose of ATM machines?

Economics

Government
Citizenship

Fast Fact 14

Kofi Annan, of Ghana, became the seventh Secretary General of the United Nations in 1997.

When was the United Nations founded, and for what purpose?

Fast Fact 15

The dog, which is descended from the wolf, was the first animal to be tamed.

How are domesticated animals different from wild animals?

Culture

Geography

Fast Fact 16

Unlike every other continent on Earth, Antarctica has no official standard time zones.

Why were time zones established, and how many are there?

Fast Fact 17

Enheduanna, an Akkadian high priestess, is the first *known* author in history. Her hymns to the goddess Inanna include details about her own life.

Who was Enheduanna's father and what was his role in Akkad?

History

Economics

Fast Fact 18

In ancient times, the Lydians were the first to develop coin money in their region of the world.

How did the invention of money affect trade?

Fast Fact 19

After the Roman republic collapsed in about 30 B.C., there wasn't another republic in Europe for more than 1,100 years. At that time, new republics began to appear in northern Italy.

What were some titles for Roman government officials during the republic?

Government Citizenship

Culture

Fast Fact 20

Native Australians began using boomerangs as early as 5000 B.C.

What is the name of the people who were already living in Australia when the Europeans arrived?

Fast Fact 21

In 1991 thousands of sneakers fell off a cargo ship northeast of Hawaii. Scientists took the opportunity to study ocean currents by locating the shoes as they washed ashore.

Why might scientists want to learn about ocean currents?

Geography

History

Fast Fact 22

Marshmallows date as far back as 2000 B.C., when Egyptians boiled the root-pulp of the marsh mallow plant with honey and let it cool. But the candy was reserved for gods and royalty!

In ancient Egyptian history, during which kingdom would marshmallow candy have been made?

Fast Fact 23

Diamonds from the African country of Namibia are considered more valuable than diamonds from any other country in Africa.

What are the leading exports of Namibia?

Economics

Government
Citizenship

Fast Fact 24

The first democracy was formed in Athens in 510 B.C. Only free adult male citizens—less than 10 percent of the population—were allowed to vote.

What are three modern countries that have democratic forms of government?

Fast Fact 25

The first coffee drinkers lived in Arabia in about A.D. 1000. Muslim philosopher and physician Avicenna introduced the drink, thinking that it could be used as a medicine.

What advancements did the Muslims make in medicine?

Culture

Geography

Fast Fact 26

A volcano on the island of Krakatoa, near Java, erupted on August 27, 1883. The eruption was so loud that people heard it nearly 3,000 miles away.

The island of Java is part of what nation?

Fast Fact 27

In the 1970s archaeologists found 3.5-million-year-old human-like bones in Ethiopia. They named their find *Lucy* after the Beatles' song "Lucy in the Sky with Diamonds."

Bones are not the only artifacts of archaeological interest in Ethiopia. What twelfth- and thirteenth-century artifacts can be attributed to Zagwe king, Lalibela?

History

Economics

The ancient Romans developed the concrete we use today.

What did the ancient Romans make out of concrete?

Fast Fact 29

Haile Selassie I, emperor of Ethiopia from 1930 to 1974, was called "the Conquering Lion" for his defeat of Ethiopia's enemies.

To what dynasty of rulers did Selassie belong?

Government Citizenship

Culture

Fast Fact 30

The oldest printed book in the world was made in China in A.D. 868.

During what dynasty did the Chinese invent paper and ink?

Fast Fact 31

The Vikings traveled by sea from Scandinavia all the way to present-day Istanbul and Baghdad.

In what modern countries are Istanbul and Baghdad located?

Geography

Fast Fact 32

The Book of Kells is a manuscript of the Christian Gospels, hand-illustrated by Scottish monks about A.D. 800. Some of the details are so delicate they cannot be seen with the ordinary eye.

What story do the Christian Gospels tell?

Fast Fact 33

The fruit of the date palms of Oman, a country in the Middle East, are such valuable trade goods that the government maintains a list of who owns which date palm trees.

What is a trade agreement?

Economics

Government
Citizenship

Fast Fact 34

Hiawatha and the Peacemaker taught the Great Law of Peace to warring Indian nations. This law was woven into a wampum belt, which can still be read by many traditional Iroquois people.

What are some of the rules that Deganawidah, the Peacemaker, established for the Iroquois Confederacy?

Fast Fact 35

In ancient times, the Chinese used a ten-day week instead of the seven-day week used today.

How do we know about the Chinese calendar used during the Shang dynasty?

Culture

Geography

Fast Fact 36

The world's largest empire was established by the conquests of Mongol ruler Genghis Khan.

What were the easternmost and westernmost boundaries of the Mongol, or Yuan, Empire?

Fast Fact 37

Archaeology tells us a lot about the past. Before the excavations at Mohenjo-Daro and Harappa in the 1920s, those civilizations had been "lost" for nearly 4,000 years!

What else do we know about these Indus Valley civilizations?

History

Economics

Fast Fact 38

Many ancient Roman emperors had their wives portrayed on coins.

Name one wife of a Roman emperor who was portrayed on a coin.

Fast Fact 39

More than four dozen countries are ruled by monarchs today. However, many of these kings and queens are only symbolic rulers.

What are two countries ruled by monarchs today?

Government Citizenship

Culture

Fast Fact 40

The Native Americans who lived in Mesoamerica and South America were considered the best farmers in the world at the time of the Spanish conquest.

How did the Aztecs create farmland in the middle of a lake?

Fast Fact 41

Almost all of Antarctica is covered by an ice sheet that is about 6,500 feet thick.

Where does Antarctica rank among other continents in terms of area?

Geography

History

Fast Fact 42

The people of ancient Troy, which is in modern-day Turkey, wrote about raspberries. They called them *idas*, after the mountain on which they grew.

For what are the people of Troy more commonly known?

Fast Fact 43

Cowboys aren't only in the American West. Argentina is famous for the quality of its beef, and the folks who tend cattle there are known as *gauchos.*

What are some exports from Argentina?

Economics

Government
Citizenship

Fast Fact 44

Shang dynasty kings kept busy. In addition to being heads of state, they were also head priests, leaders of the military and aristocracy, and responsible for the economy.

What civilizations flourished in the rest of the world during the Shang dynasty?

Fast Fact 45

The mathematical symbols (+) and (−) have been in use for about 500 years.

The Muslim culture is credited with the development of what field of mathematics?

Culture

Geography

Fast Fact 46

More than half of the world's population lives in climate zones that have monsoons.

What happens during the monsoon season?

Fast Fact 47

Did you know that the phrase "raining cats and dogs" comes from Norse (Viking) mythology? Dogs are associated with wind, and cats with storms.

During what years did the Vikings set out to explore and conquer other lands?

History

Economics

Fast Fact 48

The country of Lithuania relies on nuclear energy. It obtains more than 77 percent of its electricity from nuclear sources.

What are some sources of hydroelectric energy?

Fast Fact 49

A *bestiarist* is a person who collects medieval books about animals.

What English medieval book was used to keep track of animals, people, and land, and for what purpose?

Government Citizenship

Culture

Fast Fact 50

The oldest European suit of armor was made about 3,200 years ago in Greece. The armor includes a helmet made of metal and boars' teeth, a chest protector, and a skirt made of metal.

What civilization was powerful in Greece at about this time?

Fast Fact 51

São Paulo is the most populous city in South America. More than 17 million people live in the São Paulo metropolitan area.

In what country is São Paulo located?

Geography

History

Fast Fact 52

There is a petroglyph, or rock painting, at Canyon de Chelly, Arizona, showing the arrival of the Spaniards on horseback.

Where have some examples of cave art been discovered?

Fast Fact 53

The demand for tulips in seventeenth-century Holland was so high that people sold their jewels, homes, and even their land to invest in the tulip industry.

What are the leading exports of the Netherlands, popularly known as Holland, today?

Economics

Fast Fact 54

Gupta emperors practiced religious tolerance. Art, literature, and sciences prospered under their rule, and Hindu and Buddhist universities attracted students from as far away as China.

About how long did the Gupta empire last?

Fast Fact 55

The first mention of soap in history was on Sumerian clay tablets from about 2500 B.C.

What was the name of the wedge-shaped writing Sumerians used on clay tablets?

Culture

Geography

Fast Fact 56

Tibet has a higher elevation than most other places around the world. The bottoms of Tibetan valleys are higher than mountains in many countries.

What is the highest mountain in the world, and where is it located?

Fast Fact 57

The main part of the Great Wall stretches more than 2,000 miles across northern China. Large portions of the wall were rebuilt under the Ming dynasty in an attempt to keep invaders out.

Which ruler, from which dynasty, began the creation of the Great Wall?

History

Economics

Fast Fact 58

Americans throw away enough office and writing paper every year to build a twelve-foot-high wall from New York to Los Angeles.

What plant did the ancient Egyptians use to make paper? What is used to make paper today?

Fast Fact 59

In seventeenth-century England, there was no freedom of the press. People who disagreed with the government and printed their views were punished.

Is there freedom of the press in the United States today? Why or why not?

Government Citizenship

Culture

Fast Fact 60

Ice cream dates back to A.D. 62. The Roman emperor Nero sent his servants up into the mountains to gather snow and ice, which were then flavored with fruit and honey.

Was Nero considered one of the great Roman emperors? Why or why not?

Fast Fact 61

At the end of his life, Columbus believed the Earth was pear-shaped. Centuries earlier the Babylonians had calculated that the Earth was shaped like an oyster!

Why do you think that people disagreed about the shape of the Earth?

Geography

History

Fast Fact 62

In curling, 42-pound polished stones are thrown or swept across ice into circular goals. The game's origins are unknown, but it has been part of Scottish culture since the 1500s.

Curling became a winter sport at the Olympic Games in 1998. What other winter sports are part of the Olympic Games?

Fast Fact 63

The Atacama Desert in northern Chile is rich in copper reserves. More than 40 percent of the world's copper production takes place there.

What is Chile's leading food export?

Economics

Government Citizenship

Fast Fact 64

Attila the Hun became a romantic legend in epic poems, but he was a real person. He was a strong leader and warlord, and the Eastern Roman Empire paid him annual tribute.

What Visigoth leader attacked Rome twice in the early fifth century?

Fast Fact 65

Clocks have not always had two hands. Before 1687, clocks were made only with an hour hand.

What Song dynasty invention improved clocks?

Culture

Geography

Fast Fact 66

Astronauts in orbit over Earth can see the light of man-made forest fires in the Amazon rain forest. People set these fires to clear the land.

On what continent is the Amazon rain forest located?

Fast Fact 67

In 1893 New Zealand became the first nation to grant women the right to vote.

During what years did women gain the right to vote in the United States, the Soviet Union, Canada, Germany, and Great Britain?

History

Economics

Fast Fact 68

Oranges, grapefruit, and other citrus fruits are Florida's most important farm products. Tomatoes are the second leading crop.

The Aztecs were the first to grow tomatoes. On what was their economy based?

Fast Fact 69

Venice was a city-state that became an empire. In the 1400s its empire included Crete, Cyprus, and parts of present-day Croatia and Italy.

Name two other important city-states in Italy at about that time.

Government Citizenship

Culture

Fast Fact 70

Zoroastrianism was the state religion of three successive Persian dynasties. Many elements of Zoroaster's teachings influenced the development of Judaism, Christianity, and Islam.

What are the followers of Zoroastrianism called today?

Fast Fact 71

The highest sand dunes in the world are located in the Namib Desert in Namibia. Some of these dunes rise more than 1,300 feet.

What countries in Africa surround Namibia?

Geography

History

Fast Fact 72

The Colossus of Rhodes, a huge bronze statue of the Greek sun god, was built about 290 B.C.

What other Wonder of the Ancient World was located in Babylon during the reign of Nebuchadnezzar II?

Fast Fact 73

It only takes five recycled plastic bottles to make enough fiberfill to stuff a ski jacket.

Plastic is a petroleum product. What are some countries that export petroleum?

Economics

Government Citizenship

Fast Fact 74

Australian citizens over the age of 18 are required by law to vote in general elections. People are fined about $20 unless they provide a good reason for failing to vote.

How old do American citizens have to be to vote in general elections?

Fast Fact 75

Citrus is first mentioned in literature about 2400 B.C.

What hero of Sumerian literature may have lived at about the same time?

Culture

Geography

Fast Fact 76

There really was a Count Dracula! He lived in an area of Romania known as Transylvania, where his castle still stands in the town of Sighisoara.

What mountain range, a continuation of the Carpathian Mountains, runs east and west near the center of Romania?

Fast Fact 77

In 1895 a student at Springfield College in Massachusetts invented *mintonette*, a net-and-ball game that later became known as volleyball.

What were the rules for the Aztec ball game?

History

Economics

Fast Fact 78

Sri Lankans made steel in monsoon-wind-powered furnaces as early as A.D. 600. The steel was a trade goods, and may have been the source of the legendary Damascus swords.

Damascus is a city in Syria. Do you think that trade between Sri Lanka and Syria was easy or difficult? Why?

Fast Fact 79

In the sixteenth-century, the Ottoman Empire was the strongest in the world. At its height, it controlled the countries of Hungary, Romania, Bosnia, and Greece, among others.

When did Greece win its independence from the Ottoman Empire?

Government Citizenship

Culture

Fast Fact 80

Easter Island is home to more than 800 carved stone heads, or *moai*. Some heads are 30 feet tall, and on average they weigh about 30,000 pounds. They are believed to represent chiefs.

Which Ethiopian kingdom constructed large stone towers that could have been built as symbols of power?

Fast Fact 81

The Inuit made technological advancements in their harsh arctic biome. To protect their eyes from snow-blindness, they carved snow goggles from bone, wood, or ivory.

Where do most Inuit live today?

Geography

History

Fast Fact 82

An earthquake in the fourteenth century caused the Pharos Lighthouse of Alexandria, Egypt, to topple into the harbor. The lighthouse lay underwater and undisturbed until the 1990s.

What else do you know about the history of Alexandria?

Fast Fact 83

After establishing contact with the West and the rest of Southeast Asia, China now has one of the fastest-growing economies in the world.

When was the Association of Southeast Asian Nations created, and for what purpose?

Economics

Government
Citizenship

Fast Fact 84

The British East India Company, founded in 1600, was a company that became a government. It controlled most of India by the late 1700s.

What empire controlled India in 1600?

Fast Fact 85

There are more than 2,700 languages in the world.

How many languages do people in your class speak?

Culture

Geography

Fast Fact 86

Vatican City, the world's smallest independent country, is only 0.17 square miles in area. The entire country could fit into New York City's Central Park almost eight times.

Vatican City is located in the middle of a major European city. What is the name of this city?

Fast Fact 87

In 1907 the *Mauritania* set a speed record crossing the Atlantic Ocean in 4 days, 19 hours. The record was not broken until 1929.

Why is the *Mauritania*'s sister ship, the *Lusitania*, famous?

History

Economics

Fast Fact 88

Although Japan lacks many natural resources and only 15 percent of its land can be farmed, the island nation became an economic superpower in the mid-twentieth century.

Under the leadership of what emperor did Japan begin to modernize its technology?

Fast Fact 89

In about A.D. 800 Charlemagne introduced his foot as a unit of measure.

Was Charlemagne a good ruler? Why?

Government Citizenship

Culture

Fast Fact 90

The oldest lighthouse still in use is the Tower of Hercules, near La Coruña, Spain. This Roman lighthouse was built around A.D. 100.

What other structures did the ancient Romans build in the lands they conquered?

Fast Fact 91

Water is the most common substance on Earth and covers more than 70 percent of the Earth's surface.

What are different kinds of bodies of water easily found on a globe?

Geography

Fast Fact 92

When Pericles rebuilt Athens, one of the buildings he had built was 237 feet long and made entirely of white marble.

This building is considered one of the greatest achievements of Greek architecture. What is the name of this building?

Fast Fact 93

When people traveled by stagecoach, a servant often went ahead to arrange for their arrival. The servant would give money "to insure promptness," which was later shortened to "tip."

When might you leave a tip?

Economics

Government
Citizenship

Fast Fact 94

In ancient Greece, the word *idiot* meant a private citizen, or one who did not take part in government.

For which type of government are the ancient Greeks known?

Fast Fact 95

In 1998, Swiss consumers ate 22.4 pounds of chocolate per person, the most in the world.

From what agricultural product did the Aztecs make chocolate?

Culture

Geography

Fast Fact 96

Between July 1971 and June 1972, 1,122 inches of snowfall were recorded at Rainier Paradise Ranger Station. That remains the record for most snow in a year in North America.

In what state is Mt. Rainier located?

Fast Fact 97

In the 1930s archaeologists discovered Biskupin, a sixth-century B.C. Polish village that had been waterlogged. Known as "the Polish Pompeii," the village has been uncovered and partially reconstructed.

Why might people compare Biskupin with Pompeii?

History

Economics

Fast Fact 98

Today international trade often takes place without money. For instance, farm equipment might be bartered for grain.

Where did international bartering take place in the Middle Ages?

Fast Fact 99

Some portraits of Napoleon Bonaparte show him with his hand tucked inside his shirt. Some historians think he may have been holding his hand over his heart. Others think he may have been holding his stomach because of indigestion.

What improvements did Napoleon make in France as emperor?

Government Citizenship

Culture

Fast Fact 100

Pure 24-karat gold is so soft that it can be shaped by hand. Most jewelry is made of 14-karat gold, which is 14 parts gold and 10 parts another mineral, usually copper.

What West African empires grew wealthy because of gold deposits in the area?

Fast Fact 101

The city of Venice is built on 120 islands in the Adriatic Sea.

What body of water does the Adriatic Sea border?

Geography

History

Fast Fact 102

In 1054 the light from an exploded star shone so brightly that it could be seen in the daytime for 23 days. Records were made of the event in Japan, China, and Europe, as well as in present-day Arizona and New Mexico.

What dynasty ruled China in 1054?

Fast Fact 103

Before 1492 European nations imported large amounts of gold from West Africa, then known as Guinea. This trade brought so much wealth to Europe that British gold coins were called guineas.

Where else did some European nations get large amounts of gold after 1492?

Economics

Fast Fact 104

Goliad, Texas, is said to be named for a famous revolutionary leader in Mexico. This leader encouraged colonists to rise up against the Spanish government.

What was the name of this leader from the village of Dolores, Mexico? Hint: Rearrange the letters of *Goliad*.

Fast Fact 105

In about A.D. 1000, a wandering group of people called Gypsies left India and traveled to Europe.

What are nomads?

Culture

Geography

Fast Fact 106

The United States purchased the Virgin Islands from Denmark in 1917 for $25 million.

Between what two bodies of water are the Virgin Islands located?

Fast Fact 107

The first people on the American continents to develop writing were the Zapotec of southern Mexico. As early as 500 B.C. they began carving symbols into stone slabs.

Who were the first people on the American continents to develop an empire?

History

Economics

Fast Fact 108

In 2001 nearly one-quarter of the oil imported into the United States came from the Persian Gulf.

What countries border the Persian Gulf?

Fast Fact 109

In Great Britain the Speaker of the House is not allowed to speak—at least not during debates. The Speaker's job is to moderate and make sure that all sides are treated fairly.

What form of government does Great Britain have?

Government Citizenship

Culture

Fast Fact 110

Beef Wellington, beef cooked in a pastry shell, was named in honor of the Duke of Wellington, who won the Battle of Waterloo in 1815.

Who did the Duke of Wellington defeat at the Battle of Waterloo?

Fast Fact 111

The Chimera, in Turkey's Taurus Mountains, is a place where methane gas seeps to the surface and bursts into flame. The fire-breathing monster of the same name from Greek mythology was said to live there.

What is the capital of present-day Turkey?

Geography

History

Fast Fact 112

The oldest legislative body in the world is the Althingi, or Alpingi, in Iceland. Vikings founded it in A.D. 930.

What were Vikings doing in present-day France at about the same time?

Fast Fact 113

Eyeglasses imported from Europe cost as much as $200 in colonial America and were worn only by wealthy, educated colonists.

Why do you think the cost of eyeglasses (adjusted for inflation) has decreased since the 1700s?

Economics

Government
Citizenship

Fast Fact 114

In the late 1400s, Ivan III declared himself "Czar of all the Russias." He called himself *czar* after the *caesars* of the Roman Empire.

What Russian czar was forced to give up his throne during the Russian Revolution?

Fast Fact 115

During the Tokugawa dynasty, the Japanese were isolated from the rest of the world but often included Western inventions in their paintings.

How did the Japanese know about Western inventions?

Culture

Fast Fact 116

Benelux is an acronym for the countries of Belgium, the Netherlands, and Luxembourg, as well as the customs union they established in 1948.

On which continent are these three countries located?

Fast Fact 117

The world's first textbook was published in Leipzig, Germany, in 1507, and the first daily newspaper in 1660, also in Leipzig.

When was the first printing press invented?

History

Economics

Fast Fact 118

During apartheid, South African coins were inscribed in English or Afrikaans and showed images referring to Dutch settlers. Now the coins are inscribed in African languages such as Zulu and Xhosa.

How did other nations show their disapproval of South African apartheid policies?

Fast Fact 119

King George I of England spoke German and French, but not English. His cabinet ministers ran the country, and the office of prime minister was created to represent the king's interests.

What was the name of the prime minister who led great Britain to victory in World War II?

Government Citizenship

Culture

Fast Fact 120

The philosopher George Santayana is famous for his saying, "Those who cannot remember the past are condemned to repeat it."

Why do you think it might be important for people today to learn from the past?

Fast Fact 121

Lake Superior is the largest freshwater body in the world.

What is the largest freshwater lake in Africa?

Geography

History

Fast Fact 122

Staronova Synagogue in Prague is the oldest surviving synagogue in Europe. Legend has it that the foundation stone is from the Second Temple in Jerusalem, destroyed in A.D. 70.

What armies destroyed Jerusalem in A.D. 70?

Fast Fact 123

In the 1350s, two wealthy banks in Florence were ruined when King Edward III of England was unable to pay back his loan.

Where might banks get the money that they use to issue loans?

Economics

Government Citizenship

Fast Fact 124

The colors of the United States flag stand for courage, truth, and justice.

What are some other symbols of the United States?

Fast Fact 125

The Italian opera composer Giuseppe Verdi became a symbol of Italian nationalism. "Viva Verdi!" was a political slogan that stood for <u>V</u>ittorio <u>E</u>manuele <u>R</u>e <u>D</u>'<u>I</u>talia, Victor Emmanuel, King of Italy.

For what other arts besides opera is Italy famous?

Culture

Geography

Fast Fact 126

More than 90 percent of Libya is desert, and the country does not have a single year-round river or lake.

Libya is closest to what major body of water?

Fast Fact 127

Through the early 1800s, shoes were made to be worn on either foot. George IV of England was the first to wear shoes made to fit each of his feet.

What event was taking place in Mexico under Agustín de Iturbide when George IV was king of England?

History

Economics

Fast Fact 128

Chinese porcelain was too fragile to transport along the Silk Road. As a result, the porcelain trade did not flourish until sea routes opened up in the seventeenth century.

What famous traveler and explorer kept journals of his travels along the Silk Road?

Fast Fact 129

The kings on playing cards represent legendary rulers. Spades show King David, clubs show Alexander the Great, hearts show Charlemagne, and Julius Caesar is the king of diamonds.

What kingdoms or empires did these kings govern?

Government Citizenship

Culture

Fast Fact 130

Japanese art influenced many famous European painters, including Vincent Van Gogh, Henri de Toulouse-Lautrec, and Edgar Degas.

In what country was Van Gogh born?

Fast Fact 131

The Atlantic Ocean is saltier than the Pacific Ocean.

What are the names of the other oceans?

Geography

History

Fast Fact 132

The chief residence of the queen of England is Windsor Castle, which was built by William the Conqueror about 1070 and made into a royal home by Henry I. The castle is located just outside of London.

For how many years was Victoria queen of England?

Fast Fact 133

After World War I, inflation caused German *Reichstag* bank notes to become so worthless that some German artists used the notes to make collages.

What are reparations?

Economics

Government
Citizenship

Fast Fact 134

Italian dictator Benito Mussolini planned to build a new Roman Empire in North Africa. He wanted the Mediterranean to become an "Italian lake."

What country did Mussolini invade in 1935 to pursue his goal?

Fast Fact 135

Spanish is not the only language spoken in Spain. Many people in the northern regions of Spain also speak a second language: Catalan, Basque, or Galician.

Why might it be helpful to know more than one language?

Culture

Geography

Fast Fact 136

There are at least 15,000 species of plants that can be found only in Colombia.

Which nations border Colombia?

Fast Fact 137

During the Napoleonic Wars, French troops were often left hungry, while Nicoll, Napoleon's horse, was always well fed. The word *pumpernickel* comes from *pain pour Nicoll,* which is French for "bread for Nicoll."

Why were the Napoleonic Wars fought?

History

Economics

Fast Fact 138

United States currency notes are made of woven linen and cotton.

What culture invented paper money?

Fast Fact 139

Until 1992 the Kingdom of Saudi Arabia had no formal constitution. Before that time, Saudi Arabia considered the Quran to be the state constitution.

Why might the Quran be used as a constitution or legal code?

Government Citizenship

Culture

Fast Fact 140

The modern food known as pizza was first made in Naples, Italy, in 1889. Its ingredients represented the Italian flag: red (tomatoes), white (mozzarella cheese), and green (basil).

When did Italy become a united nation?

Fast Fact 141

Rice cultivation alone accounts for 45 percent of Vietnam's gross national product.

What three bodies of water border Vietnam?

Geography

History

Fast Fact 142

On July 4, 1776, King George III of England wrote in his diary, "Nothing of importance happened today."

Why would King George not have known what had just happened in the American colonies?

Fast Fact 143

When mining diamonds, only one carat in every twenty-three tons of rock turns out to be a diamond.

Which countries export diamonds?

Economics

Fast Fact 144

Japanese Emperor Hirohito was the 124th holder of his title. At the time of his reign, the same family had held the throne in Japan since the sixth century A.D.

In which African country did the Solomonid dynasty hold power from the 1200s to the 1970s?

Fast Fact 145

In Africa the Tuareg people often race camels, and Berber horsemen ride to show off their skills.

In what region of Africa do the Tuaregs and Berbers live?

Culture

Geography

Fast Fact 146

The native people of Japan are Ainu. For the most part, they have become part of Japanese culture, but some small groups of Ainu still live apart on the northern Japanese island of Hokkaido.

What is the name of largest city on the island of Hokkaido?

Fast Fact 147

The Adventures of Tom Sawyer, by Mark Twain, was the first novel to be written on a typewriter.

What technology did people use to write before the invention of the typewriter?

History

Economics

Fast Fact 148

During the American Revolution, the price of corn rose 10,000 percent, the price of flour 15,000 percent, and the price of beef 33,000 percent.

What is inflation?

Fast Fact 149

After the countries of Africa were divided among European countries at the Berlin Conference in the 1880s, British imperialist Cecil Rhodes said that he would "annex the planets" if he could.

What two African countries were never colonized by a European nation?

Government Citizenship

Culture

Fast Fact 150

The musician Ravi Shankar introduced sitar music to a wide audience in Europe and the United States in the 1950s and 1960s. One of his students was George Harrison of the Beatles.

The sitar is a musical instrument of what country?

Fast Fact 151

In 1980 Mount St. Helens erupted, exploding off the top 1,314 feet of the mountain and killing at least 57 people in the state of Washington.

What major volcanic eruption occurred in A.D. 79 in Pompeii?

Geography

History

Fast Fact 152

In World War II, women made up about 8 percent of the Soviet army that fought in combat.

Who was the American commander of the U.S. Women's Army Corps during World War II?

Fast Fact 153

Money in international trade has become "virtual"! Instead of using coins and bills, individuals and banks wire money through telephone lines from one computer to another.

Which route across Asia helped the rise of international trade in the Middle Ages?

Economics

Government Citizenship

Fast Fact 154

After the U.S. occupation of Japan ended in 1952, Japan's constitution of 1947 went into effect. The 1947 constitution was a revision of the 1889 Meiji constitution.

For whom or what is the Meiji constitution named?

Fast Fact 155

India and South Korea both celebrate Independence Day on August 15.

From which countries did India and South Korea win their independence?

Culture

Geography

Fast Fact 156

In 1499 Spanish explorers in the Americas came across a village built on poles above the water. They named the area *Venezuela,* or " Little Venice," because the village reminded them of buildings along the water in Venice.

What large body of water borders Venezuela to the north?

Fast Fact 157

The Boxer Rebellion received its name from its association with an ancient Chinese martial art called *kung fu*.

What happened during the Boxer Rebellion of 1898–1900?

History

Economics

Fast Fact 158

One side of a euro coin has a European design and the other side has a design created by each member country. Euro coins can be used in any of the member countries.

When was the euro put into circulation?

Fast Fact 159

Trizonia was the term used for the combined British, French, and U.S. occupation zones in Germany after World War II.

Which country controlled the zone where Berlin was located?

Government Citizenship

Culture

Fast Fact 160

Pizza first became popular in the United States after World War II. Soldiers returning from the war craved the pizza they had eaten in Italy.

What are some other popular foods that are not native to the United States?

Fast Fact 161

Mt. Vesuvius is the only active volcano on the mainland of Europe.

Where are some other historically active volcanoes located?

Geography

History

Fast Fact 162

Israel offered to make Albert Einstein its president in 1952. He turned down the offer.

Who was Israel's first prime minister?

Fast Fact 163

One of the world's largest petroleum companies got its start in 1833 in London, trading oriental sea shells.

Where are most of the major oil fields located?

Economics

Government
Citizenship

Fast Fact 164

When Queen Elizabeth I of England lost some of her teeth, she stuffed rags into her mouth to prevent the appearance of hollow cheeks.

What great changes did Queen Elizabeth I's reign bring to England?

Fast Fact 165

Monks in medieval England kept bees. When the Church of England was created, Catholic monasteries were outlawed, which led to a shortage of honey. This shortage created a demand for sugar from the New World colonies.

What do we call the communities in which nuns live?

Culture

Geography

Fast Fact 166

Bangkok's name is the longest in the world. Translated, it means "City of Angels, Greatest of Cities, Immortal Precious Jewel, All Powerful, Ancient, Nine-Jeweled Heavenly City, Built by Vishnukarma, Architect of Indra."

Bangkok is located near which gulf?

Fast Fact 167

In 1972 the *Apollo 17* crew made the last human visit to the moon.

When did the first human visit to the moon occur?

History

Economics

Fast Fact 168

Until the twentieth century, gold dust was the main currency for the Asante, a group of people who live in present-day Ghana. The dust was weighed on scales with brass weights.

What problem might the Asante have faced with using gold dust instead of gold objects?

Fast Fact 169

Greece was a monarchy until 1974; now it is a parliamentary republic.

What is another country that is governed by a parliament?

Government Citizenship

Culture

Fast Fact 170

Japanese filmmaker Akira Kurosawa's 1985 film *Ran* was inspired by William Shakespeare's play *King Lear*.

What Japanese author wrote *The Tale of Genji*?

Fast Fact 171

In 1997 a U.S. robot controlled from Earth explored the surface of Mars.

How might people on Earth have controlled the robot on Mars?

Geography

History

Fast Fact 172

Queen Berengaria, wife of the British king Richard the Lion-Hearted, never set foot in England. King Richard himself only spent a total of about one year of his reign there.

What battles were Christian leaders across western Europe, including King Richard, fighting at this time?

Fast Fact 173

In 2001 Americans spent nearly $2 billion on Halloween candy, and just more than $1 billion on candy for Valentine's Day.

What are some ways to celebrate your favorite holiday without spending a lot of money?

Economics

Fast Fact 174

The Evian Agreements came out of a town in France famous for its water. The agreements ended the Algerian War of Independence in 1962.

Against whom did the Algerians fight for independence?

Fast Fact 175

People who lived on the Arabian Peninsula were referred to as *Arabs.* Today, anyone who speaks Arabic is an Arab, including 150 million people in the Middle East and Africa.

Why did the Arabic language spread so far from the Arabian Peninsula?

Culture

Geography

Fast Fact 176

The Gulf of Mexico, with more than 3,000 miles of shoreline, is the largest gulf in the world.

What are three southeast coast states that border the Gulf of Mexico?

Fast Fact 177

When the *Apollo 11* crew made the first moon landing in 1969, they landed in a place named the Sea of Tranquility.

What are the names of the first people to have walked on the moon?

History

Economics

Fast Fact 178

In 1997 Americans spent nearly $24 billion on computers and computer equipment.

Why are computers an important part of the economy in the United States?

Fast Fact 179

In January 2002, the province of Newfoundland changed its name to the province of Newfoundland and Labrador.

In what country is the province of Newfoundland and Labrador located?

Government Citizenship

Culture

Fast Fact 180

The South American country with the greatest land area does not use Spanish as its official language. The people there speak Portuguese.

What is this country?

Fast Facts Answers

1. Europe, Africa, and Asia
2. about 10,000 years ago
3. Queen Isabella of Spain funded Columbus's search for a westward passage to spice-rich Asia because she wanted to spread Christianity and compete with Portugal for wealth.
4. Inca runners carried the messages on trails throughout the empire.
5. The summer and winter Olympic Games alternate every two years.
6. about 15,000
7. in southwestern Asia in an area called the Fertile Crescent
8. Women boiled the cocoons of silkworms to get silk fibers, and then wove cloth from these fibers.
9. Roman soldiers had citizenship papers, some of which were copied onto pieces of bronze.
10. Answers will vary but may include silk, paper, and porcelain.
11. Iran, Turkmenistan, Kazakhstan, Russia, and Azerbaijan
12. Hannibal
13. to provide convenient banking services, such as cash withdrawal or money transfer between accounts
14. 1945; to promote world peace and economic and social welfare
15. Domesticated animals that are tamed rely on humans for survival.
16. to standardize timekeeping; 24
17. The Akkadian king Sargon founded the kingdom of Akkad and joined Sumer and Akkad, creating the world's first empire.
18. Money made trading easier because it had value that was guaranteed by the king or government.
19. consuls, dictators, and tribunes

20. the Aborigines
21. Answers may include that currents affect weather, deep-sea fishing, and shipping lanes.
22. the Middle Kingdom
23. Answers may include diamonds, copper, gold, zinc, and lead.
24. Answers may include the United States, Mexico, France, England, and Argentina, among others.
25. A Muslim scholar wrote an encyclopedia of medicine, and Muslim doctors discovered that blood circulates throughout the body.
26. Indonesia
27. the eleven churches Zagwe king Lalibela had carved out of solid rock
28. roads
29. the Solomonid dynasty
30. Han dynasty
31. Turkey and Iraq
32. the story of the life of Jesus, founder of the Christian religion
33. an agreement with rules about the exchange of goods between countries
34. Each tribe had a vote; the confederacy could not act unless all tribes were in agreement.
35. We know about this calendar because of inscriptions found on oracle bones.
36. easternmost: the Pacific coast of Asia; westernmost: the Danube River in Europe
37. Answers may include that they had a system of writing, farmed and stored grain, worked with metal and pottery, wove cotton, traded and sold goods, and had complex architecture.
38. Empress Eudocia
39. Answers may include England, Spain, and Jordan, among others.
40. They anchored wicker baskets to the bottom of the lake, filled the baskets with mud, and cut plants to form islands.
41. fifth largest
42. Answers may include aspects of the Trojan War, including the wooden horse.
43. wheat, manufactured goods, corn, oilseed

44. the New Kingdom in Egypt, the Olmec in Central America, and Mycenae in Europe
45. algebra
46. Nearly all of the yearly precipitation falls at this time. Also, off the coast of China, monsoon winds blow from southwest to northeast in summer, and northeast to southwest in winter.
47. 800–1100
48. rapidly flowing rivers, dams, or waterfalls
49. the *Domesday Book*; as a census and to determine the basis of taxes
50. Mycenae
51. Brazil
52. Spain (Altamira Cave), France (Lascaux and Chauvet Caves), Portugal, Australia, and South Africa
53. machinery and equipment, flowers, chemicals
54. about 200 years
55. cuneiform
56. Mount Everest, near the border of Nepal
57. Shi Huangdi, of the Qin dynasty
58. papyrus; trees
59. Yes; the Constitution of the United States provides for this freedom.
60. No, because Nero poisoned his stepbrother and murdered his wife and mother.
61. Answers may include that no one had circumnavigated the globe yet, or that science had not advanced enough to make accurate calculations that people trusted.
62. Answers may include luge, skiing, bobsledding, and figure skating, among others.
63. fish
64. Alaric
65. the chain-drive mechanism for celestial clocks
66. South America
67. between 1917 and 1920
68. agriculture
69. Florence and Milan
70. Parsis
71. Angola, Zambia, Botswana, and South Africa

72. the Hanging Gardens of Babylon
73. Answers may include Algeria, Canada, Colombia, Iran, and Saudi Arabia, among others.
74. 18
75. Gilgamesh
76. the Transylvanian Alps
77. Each team tried to knock a heavy rubber ball through a stone ring without allowing the ball to touch the ground or their hands.
78. Answers will vary but should indicate an understanding of the distance and variety of routes possible.
79. in 1830
80. the kingdom of Axum
81. in the Canadian territory of Nunavut, which means "Our Land" in the Inuktitut language
82. Answers may include that it was founded by Alexander the Great, and that its library was once the greatest in the world.
83. in 1967, to promote economic cooperation among five Southeast Asian nations
84. The Mogul Empire
85. Answers will vary.
86. Rome, Italy
87. The *Lusitania* was a British ship that was sunk by a German submarine during World War I. Nearly 1,200 people died. The sinking of the *Lusitania* helped push the United States into the war.
88. Meiji
89. Answers will vary but should show an understanding of his support of culture and learning, as well as his methods of rule and conquest.
90. Answers will include aqueducts, roads, and buildings.
91. Answers may include oceans, rivers, sounds, lakes, bays, gulfs, channels, and seas.
92. the Parthenon

93. Answers may include tips for a server at a restaurant, hotel workers, or a skycap at an airport.
94. democratic
95. cacao beans
96. Washington
97. Both cities were covered up by a natural phenomenon and discovered more-or-less intact.
98. along trade routes
99. He strengthened the French government and restored order. He also established a new system of laws called the Napoleonic Code.
100. Answer should include the empires of Mali and Ghana.
101. the Ionian Sea
102. the Song dynasty
103. the Americas
104. Father Miguel Hidalgo
105. people who move from place to place to have food or pasture for their cattle
106. the Caribbean Sea and the Atlantic Ocean
107. the Aztec
108. Kuwait, Iran, Saudi Arabia, Iraq, Oman, United Arab Emirates, and Qatar
109. constitutional monarchy
110. Napoleon
111. Ankara
112. They were being converted to Christianity and becoming church leaders. Under William the Conqueror, the Vikings invaded England and southern Italy.
113. Manufacturing of eyeglasses within the country began, which meant they could be produced cheaper and bypass tariff costs.
114. Czar Nicholas II
115. The Japanese continued to trade with the Dutch during their period of isolation.
116. Europe

117. in the 1450s
118. They placed sanctions, or penalties, on South Africa.
119. Winston Churchill
120. Students should give examples from history to back up their replies.
121. Lake Victoria
122. Roman armies
123. from customer deposits and from investments
124. Answers may include the Statue of Liberty, the Liberty Bell, the bald eagle, and so on.
125. Answers may include painting or sculpture.
126. Its northern border is the Mediterranean Sea.
127. Mexico fought against Spain to gain independence and won it in 1821.
128. Marco Polo
129. Israel, Macedonia, Kingdom of the Franks, Roman Empire
130. the Netherlands
131. the Arctic Ocean and the Indian Ocean
132. 64 years, from 1837 to 1901
133. payment for war losses
134. Ethiopia
135. Answers may include being able to communicate with more people or being better prepared for job opportunities.
136. Ecuador, Peru, Brazil, Venezuela, and Panama
137. Napoleon wanted to restore the Roman Empire, and the nations of Europe fought successfully to prevent his conquest.
138. the Chinese
139. The Quran states many guidelines for everyday living, such as the Five Pillars and a code on business affairs.
140. in 1861
141. the Gulf of Tonkin, the South China Sea, and the Gulf of Thailand

142. In 1776 it took a long time for information to travel from the United States to England.
143. Answers may include, among others, Angola, the Democratic Republic of the Congo, Liberia, and Sri Lanka.
144. Ethiopia
145. Sapporo
146. the Pyrenees
147. paper and a pen or pencil
148. the rapid increase in prices
149. Ethiopia and Liberia
150. India
151. the eruption of Mount Vesuvius
152. Oveta Culp Hobby
153. the Silk Road
154. Meiji was the first emperor of what became the Meiji restoration (the restoration of the emperor) in Japan.
155. India won independence from Great Britain; South Korea won independence from Japan.
156. the Caribbean Sea
157. A powerful Chinese group known as "the Boxers" wanted to destroy all foreign influences. A European army defeated the Boxers.
158. 2002
159. the Soviet Union
160. Answers will vary.
161. Answers may include, among others, Mt. St. Helens in WA, Mt. Kilauea in HI, and volcanoes in Mexico.
162. David Ben-Gurion
163. in the Middle East, along the Gulf of Mexico, and in Siberia
164. During Queen Elizabeth's reign, England became a world sea power. She also promoted the arts.
165. convents
166. the Gulf of Thailand

167. July 1969
168. Students might suggest that dust blows away, and that it can be difficult to store and transport.
169. Answers may include Great Britain, Canada, Australia, and so on.
170. Lady Murasaki Shikibu
171. They may have used computers and satellites.
172. the Crusades
173. Answers will vary.
174. France
175. Because the only acceptable version of the Quran was in Arabic; the Arabic language spread along with Islam.
176. Answers may include Texas, Louisiana, Mississippi, Alabama, and Florida.
177. Neil Armstrong and Edwin Aldrin
178. Answers may include that computers are a growing part of commerce and everyday life; they shape how we communicate with other people and how we learn.
179. Canada
180. Brazil